FAITHFUL
MEN AND WOMEN
OF THE
BIBLE

AUTHOR: GOD
HIS SERVANT: REV. DR. SUE PERRY

WestBow Press books may be ordered through booksellers or by contacting:

WestBow Press
A Division of Thomas Nelson & Zondervan
1663 Liberty Drive
Bloomington, IN 47403
www.westbowpress.com
1 (866) 928-1240

Because of the dynamic nature of the Internet, any web addresses or links contained in this book may have changed since publication and may no longer be valid. The views expressed in this work are solely those of the author and do not necessarily reflect the views of the publisher, and the publisher hereby disclaims any responsibility for them.

Any people depicted in stock imagery provided by Getty Images are models, and such images are being used for illustrative purposes only.
Certain stock imagery © Getty Images.

ISBN: 978-1-9736-9695-7 (sc)
ISBN: 978-1-9736-9696-4 (e)

Library of Congress Control Number: 2020912864

Print information available on the last page.

WestBow Press rev. date: 07/16/2020

WESTBOW
PRESS®
A DIVISION OF THOMAS NELSON
& ZONDERVAN

All glory, honor and praise to God the Father, His beloved Son our Savior and to the Holy Spirit. Three in One God now and forever.

With special thanks to my God child Jane Perry for helping me navigate the computer and to my friend Brenda Hudson for her constant support and prayers.
A special thanks to my husband for his support.

HANNAH AND SAMUEL

There once lived a woman named Hannah. Hannah loved God and her husband.

Although Hannah and her husband had been married several years, Hannah did not have any children.

Hannah's husband was also married to Peninnah. Peninnah had many children.

Because Hannah did not have children, Peninnah was very mean to her.

Hannah was so sad (because she did not have children) that sometimes she cried and would not eat her supper.

One day, Hannah and her husband Elkanah went to the temple of the Lord to offer sacrifices and to pray.

Hannah was so sad that she wept as she prayed for God to give her a child.

Hannah then made a promise that if God would give her a son, she would keep him holy, AND she would bring him back to the temple to serve God all his life.

Now Eli the priest who was standing in the temple saw Hannah praying. She did not make any sound because she was praying silently. However, the priest thought she was drunk! He told her to stop drinking.

Hannah replied that she was not drunk but was praying from her heart, telling God how sad she was. Therefore, the priest told her to go home, saying that God would give her what she asked for, and although the priest did not know that it was for a male child, God knew.

God heard Hannah's prayer, as He always hears our prayers, and he gave her a son, Samuel.

When Samuel was still very young, Hannah kept her promise to God and took the boy to the temple. She told the priest that Samuel was the boy she had prayed for and that she was fulfilling her vow to God and bringing the child to the temple to serve the Lord as long as he lived.

One night after Eli the priest had gone to bed, Samuel laid down to rest. Suddenly, he heard someone calling his name.

Samuel ran to Eli and told him that he had heard him calling him.

However, Eli told him he was mistaken and to go back to bed.

So Samuel went to lie down.

Again, he heard someone calling his name.

Samuel got up and went to the priest. Again, he told the priest that he had heard someone calling his name.

Eli once again told him to go back to bed.

Samuel obeyed.

The third time, Samuel heard his name called.

And he went to the priest and told him.

Then Eli the priest believed that it was God calling Samuel! He told Samuel to go lie down and if he heard his name called again he was to answer that he was listening.

Once again, Samuel lay down, however, this time when his name was called, he did what the priest told him to do.

He prayed and listened and obeyed. God was with him all his life and all the people knew Samuel was a prophet of the Lord.

ESTHER AND MORDECAI

Once many years ago, there was a man named Mordecai. He had a cousin, Hadassah, that is Esther.

Because Esther's mother and father had died, Mordecai adopted her as his daughter and she went to live with him.

Esther was very beautiful.

One day, the king sent out an edict (that is an order) that all the young women (girls) were to be brought to his harem (that is where the women lived).

You see, the king was looking for a new wife and he was going to choose one from among those girls.

So, the king's men went from place to place gathering all the young women and taking them back to the palace. And Esther was one of those who were taken to the palace.

Every girl was given special beauty treatments to prepare her to meet the king.

However, Esther was especially liked by Hegai, the guard who was in charge of the girls and he gave her the best place in the harem. He even gave her seven maids! WOW!

Now Esther and Mordecai were Jews. However, Mordecai told Esther not to tell anyone.

Each day, Mordecai would walk past the front of the court of the harem to see how Esther was doing.

Finally, after 12 months of receiving special treatments of oil and perfumes and cosmetics (makeup) each girl went to meet the king.

Each girl was given whatever she wanted to take from the harem (what she thought would make her more beautiful to the king.)

After she left the king, she did not go back to him unless he called her by name.

Finally, it was Esther's turn to meet the king. Unlike the other girls, she did not ask for anything special to take with her.

The king loved Esther more than any of the girls and he made her his queen!

One day, Mordecai was sitting by the king's gate. That is where much of the business was conducted in those days.

While Mordecai was sitting there he heard two of the king's servants making a plan to kill the king!

Mordecai quickly told queen Esther and she told the king and both men were hanged.

Mordecai saved the king's life by telling Esther about the plot to kill him and it was written in a very special book.

All the important things that happened in the kingdom were written in this book so no one would forget but the king did forget.

Some time later, the king promoted an evil man named Haman over all the other officials in the kingdom. All the king's servants bowed down before Haman because the king had ordered it to be done, except Mordecai.

When the king's servants asked Mordecai why he did not bow down, he told them that he was a Jew. Jews only bow to the Lord God.

Unfortunately, the servants told Haman that Mordecai would not bow down to him and that Mordecai was a Jew.

Haman became very, very angry and decided to destroy Mordecai and all the Jews throughout the entire kingdom! So Haman created an evil plot to destroy those he considered his enemies.

Then Haman went to the king and told him that there were certain people of the kingdom who did not obey the king's laws.

He told the king that they needed to be destroyed and a law needed to be made saying when and where this would happen.

The king called his secretaries and they wrote that awful law and it was sealed with the king's ring which made it official and could not be changed.

Then the new law was sent out into the kingdom to all the governors and officials that on a certain day, the 12th day of a certain month, they were to kill all the Jews both young and old and to take all their possessions for themselves.

When they learned of this terrible law, the people were confused. What had happened? Why were they to be killed? What had they done?

Wherever the law was sent the people were very, very upset, crying and fasting (refusing to eat.)

When Mordecai learned of the law, he was greatly distressed, he tore his clothes and put on sackcloth and ashes (that is what they did in those days when they were really, really, upset or sad).

He went throughout the city crying and even up to the king's gate.

When Esther's maids told her about Mordecai, she became very worried and sent clothes for Mordecai to put on, but he would not do it.

Then Esther sent one of her servants to find out why Mordecai was unhappy and Mordecai told him about the horrible new law. He even gave him a copy of the law to show Esther and asked her to go to the king and beg him to spare (save) the Jews from destruction.

Esther's servant told her all he had learned and that Mordecai wanted her to speak to the king. But Esther knew there was a law that said if anyone went to the king without being called by the king, they were to be put to death.

Unless, the king held out his golden scepter to them.

So Esther sent that message to Mordecai.

Mordecai sent another message to Esther and reminded her that she too would be killed with all the other Jews if this horrible thing happened.

He also told her that perhaps this was why she became queen, to save her people from death.

Then Esther told Mordecai to gather all the people together and have them fast (not eat or drink) for 3 days and that she and her maids would do the same. Then she would go to the king.

Fasting and praying was what the people did in the time of crisis. Only God can solve some problems and this was one of them.

Mordecai obeyed Esther and told the people what they were to do.

Then on the third day, Esther put on her royal robes and went to see the king.

The king was happy to see her, held out his golden scepter to her and asked her what she wanted.

Esther told the king that she would like him to come to a banquet that she had made for him and he was to bring Haman!

At the banquet the king once again asked Esther what she wanted and assured her that he would grant her wish.

Esther told the king that she would like him to come again the next day to another banquet, with Haman. Then she would tell him her request.

Haman was excited and very happy. He was the only one invited to accompany the king to a banquet held by the queen.

However, when he saw Mordecai, who of course did not bow before him, he became angry and went home to tell his wife and all his friends.

Together they decided that a very high gallows should be built and Mordecai should be hung on it! That made Haman happy and he had the gallows built.

Meanwhile, back at the palace, the king could not sleep and so he decided he would look at the book of records.

When he read the part about Mordecai saving his life, he asked what had been done for Mordecai in return. He was told nothing had been done.

By this time it was early morning and the king said who is in the courtyard? It was Haman.

So the king sent for him and told him that he wanted to honor Mordecai by putting a royal robe and crown on him, to have him ride on horseback through the city and have Haman proclaim that this is what the king was doing to honor Mordecai.

Haman did what the king ordered but he was not happy. You see he thought the king was going honor him, not his enemy Mordecai.

Later that day, Haman went with the king to the banquet held by Esther.

Once again, the king asked Esther what she desired and that is when she begged the king to save her life and the lives of her people.

The king was confused. Who would dare kill the queen?

It was Haman!

The king was so angry he stood up and went into the palace garden. However, Haman stayed with the queen to beg her to save his life. He even threw himself on the couch where the queen was sitting!

When the king returned and saw Haman, he became even angrier.

Then the servants told the king that Haman had ordered a very tall gallows to be built and that Haman was going to have Mordecai hung on it. So, the king ordered them to hang Haman on that very same gallows and they did. And all that he owned was given to Esther which she gave to Mordecai.

Then at the request of Queen Esther, the king issued an order that all the Jews could defend themselves against any and all people who might attack them.

Thus, God saved His people and to this day the people celebrate on a special day called Purim.

SHADRACH, MESHACH AND ABEDNEGO

There was a king named Nebuchadnezzar. One day the king decided to make a very, very big (approximately 90' tall and very, very wide (approximately 90') golden statue.

Then he sent word to all the governors, counselors, treasurers, judges, and other officials of the land to come and see the statue.

It was announced that all the people of the land were to fall down and worship the idol when they heard the sound of a harp, flute and other instruments.

If they did not fall down and worship the statue they would be thrown into a fiery furnace!

So, when the people heard the sound of the flute, the harp and other instruments, most of them fell down and worshipped the idol--most of them, not all of them.

Among the people, were three Jews named Shadrach, Meshach and Abednego. They served God and only God. And God's people are not to worship anyone or thing except Him.

There were certain men who served the king, who were jealous of Shadrach, Meshach and Abednego. They went to the king and told him that there were Jews who did not fall down and worship the gold image; therefore they should be thrown into the fiery furnace.

This made Nebuchadnezzar furious and he gave the command to bring the three men to him.

When they arrived, the king asked them if it was true that they would not bow before the gold image and that they did not serve his gods.

He told them he would give them one more chance to bow before the image when they heard the music of the instruments. And if they did not, he would have them thrown into the fiery furnace.

However, they could not bow before anyone or thing other than the One true God that they served.

So they answered the king and told him that God was capable of saving them no matter what happened to them. But no matter, they would not bow to the image nor would they serve false gods.

This made the king so angry that he ordered his servants to make the fiery furnace seven times hotter than usual!

Then he ordered his strong men of his army to tie up Shadrach, Meshach and Abednego and throw them into the fiery furnace.

And so it was done.

The fire was so hot it even killed the men who threw the three into the furnace.

All of a sudden the king was astonished because he could see the three men, no longer bound, walking around and with them was another person who looked like the Son of God!

The king ordered the three to come out of the furnace and they did. They were not harmed in anyway.

Then the king blessed the One true God and made a law that no one was to say anything against the God of Shadrach, Meshach and Abednego because there is no other God like Him.

God is always faithful.

NAOMI AND RUTH

There was a man named Elimelech. He lived in Bethlehem with his wife Naomi and two sons.

Unfortunately, there was a famine in the land. There was no food. So, they went to live in a country called Moab.

After some time, Elimelech died.

The two sons each got married. One of the wives was named Orpah and the other was Ruth.

Then the two sons died.

Naomi had heard that there was no longer a famine in Bethlehem so she decided to return to her home.

She called Naomi and Ruth to her and explained that it was time for her to leave and that they should each return to their previous families.

This did not make the women happy. They cried and said that they wanted to remain with Naomi. But she said no.

Again they were very sad and Orpah said good-by to Naomi and returned to her family.

However, Ruth would not leave. She begged Naomi to let her go with her to Bethlehem. She declared that she would go wherever Naomi went and that she would worship Naomi's God.

So Naomi relented and they set off together for Bethlehem.

Some time later, Ruth asked Naomi if she could go out into the fields and gather grain for their food. Naomi agreed and Ruth left.

There was among the people a man who was actually a distant relative of Naomi. His name was Boaz and it was his field that Ruth went to gather grain.

When Boaz found out who Ruth was, he instructed his men to leave extra grain for her and to be sure no one bothered her.

Then he spoke to Ruth and told her who he was and that he was glad she was helping his relative Naomi. He also told her to only gather grain in his field. She agreed and was very happy.

He even shared his lunch with Ruth!

That night when Ruth returned home, Naomi asked where she had been that day and Ruth told her about Boaz and all that had transpired.

Naomi was very happy and explained that Boaz was a relative.

One day Naomi told Ruth that it was time for her to remarry and that she should go and speak to Boaz. She did and he agreed.

They were married and they had a son, his name was Obed.

They were faithful and God delivered and blessed them.

These are just some of the faithful men and women of God. There are many others such as Miriam, Moses, Joseph, Gideon, Abraham, Mary and Joseph.

However, always remember the most faithful is the Son of God, Jesus the Messiah, who gave His life for ours.

Sources include:

NKJV Study Bible, Copyright 1997 by Thomas Nelson, Inc.

and

The Complete Jewish Study Bible, Copyright 2016 by Hendrickson Publishers

Rev. Perry and her husband Bill, retired Navy, live in North Carolina. They have 7 children, 26 grandchildren, 6 great grandchildren and 2 more on the way.

They are blessed and give all the glory to God.

Printed in the United States
By Bookmasters